I0756376

FINISHING LINE PRESS
www.finishinglinepress.com

A Harvest of Days

poems by

Alex Missall

Finishing Line Press
Georgetown, Kentucky

A Harvest of Days

ISBN 979-8-89990-360-1 First Edition

Publisher: Leah Huete de Maines
Editor: Christen Kincaid
Cover Art: Alex Missall
Author Photo: Obscura Photography
Cover Design: Elizabeth Maines McCleavy

Order online: www.finishinglinepress.com
also available on amazon.com

Author inquiries and mail orders:
Finishing Line Press
PO Box 1626
Georgetown, Kentucky 40324
USA

Contents

For

Kishma

Poetaster

From the chair beside mine,
my niece
had been cracking
a variety of nuts
out of the big,
wooden bowl
between us.
At one point,
she looked over
and asked, “What’s a poem?”
The problem, then,
was my response
that wandered
into a dawning mixture
of beauty and logic,
as if I were searching
for the mad sculptor
who had drug
his gold aurora
across a morning’s
horizon of forgotten dark—
beyond the rubble
of my own
imitating light,
which repeated back,
“A poem?”

Anamnesis

Aphorism #1

"I do not seek, I find."
—Pablo Picasso

While I trek the morning
with my father,
who is hoping
to find—
or rather—the lost

orphanage we're searching for
somewhere in this forest
behind his home,
he claims to have found
years prior.

Once through the thrash,
we do not find it,
but emerge onto land
to trespass across
an opening of home and barn,

then wander down
the privation of a fence line,
which we follow
as if toward
an Unfound.

After empty circularity,
when we stumble back
upon town and sidewalk
outside the sprawling
grounds of a school,

I find that there's always
only the impossibility
of what we seek,
the ironical exasperation
in discovering such an impossibility.

Up North

I

Wind from yesterday blows into morning,
off a lake blanketed
in an impartial tick of Time.

A coffeemaker drips.

The open windows permit,
as if an ego uncoiling
ruminations
of a tide.

II

The creaks here are ohms.
Sighing floorboards.
Warped groans.

There's the loon's wail,
then a faint thrumming
which grows:

a last boat flees
as a frayed thought
across the horizon's curve.

III

Morning, unbroken,
continues into afternoon, then dusk,
repeating, repeating
as if cleansing the self
of complexities.

Sometimes,
you'll hear chestnuts fall
fat and rattle the aluminum
of the shed.

You can sense a distance
between the light and the dark
lessen.

Possibility of an Old Lady

The plastic chair is empty,
another chair turned over—
like a new season—
onto the white cellar door.

Two terra cotta pots
are full of bright red flowers,
a cigarette butt is blown
to this sidewalk.

Asylum

And the light and wind and leaves now
before eventual
winter.

And the light and wind and leaves
now from a convalescing window
channel the stranger's
sense of unreality,
which is a conflicted
nature of mine
withdrawing
the reflection of a draft
of another self,
a past letter torn out
and mailed.

*

At that place,
when becoming untangled of silence,
I had tried to grasp
at years of our confounded feeling
in the sparse syllables
of an image sent
away.

After a timeless parenthesis,
before leaving there,
I called from a phone
on a table against a wall,
and you were at a pool somewhere
and said you had received my haiku
then hung up.

The Eternal Change I Wait For To Untire

As if a hallway abandoned
by people having left
for the square room of horizon
trailing out a far,
opened end,
the leaves left behind
sweep across this in-between
patterned by green growth under trees,
the yellow and green
overhanging from branches,
or other fallings,
alive still with color,
cover the corridor
of earth completely.

From the logic
of a bench
built before this,
I watch waves of wind
rattle and rush foliage.
Beneath appearances,
the eternal change
I wait for to untire
is an awe and ache
felt, while resting,
toward the mystery
of fate's flux,
which exists seemingly beyond
all such cycles of season and self.

Aftersound

And there's the current to the soul's definition
dividing the past and the future,
as if it were those immaterial moments
when walking by here
in the hot, vacuous whorls
of a summer afternoon.
Then, the group of friends ran out
beyond the shadowplay
of a shoreline,
into a swimming hole,
whose shallows remain
at a distance still.
While crunching this gravelly
plane above the river,
the path persists ahead
into the yellow
of leaves
over ground and trees,
the entrance into forest
mixed with primitive light,
light yellowing,
and the aftersound of laughter,
through wind, faintly heard again.

The Yesterdays of the Clock While Housesitting

I'll somehow lose
self or season here
where watching wind
take last leaves
from the transient
tree.

Like breaths,
broken vines
hang off
the rusted fence;
the garden's stone bath
collects with rainwater.

*

After this muted storm,
the cuckoo clock's
cuckoos sound inside,
their temporal wormhole
remaining three minutes
behind.

*

With the finalizing light of dusk,
the two dogs follow
behind me
down the long drive,
so as to retrieve
a newspaper's

lost enchainment of yesterdays.

The Passing That Never Is

A congregation of theorists
drag conspiring bicycles
from a
clearing

(near the gnarled tree
with footings
that lead to knotted,
windless ropes hanging from limbs
out of season
over a river).

When walking by,
after the faith I've filled with philosophies,
this flash's extension
from the friends
riding off
is a resetting back
to what materializes,
photographlike in the air ahead,
of a thin path
through a wood
one neighborhood boy
discovered, then followed
to a splintered shelter,
which became place
to all logic
unrivaled in
contradiction.

This escaping an afterimage
turning where the path ends
before a road running
between a distant rolling
cemetery and a transiency
being solely mine
sometime when returning
to the vacant clearing and the tree and the river
which exists as part to a passing
that never
is.

The Pendulum of Night

Just as the strange
can illuminate things complex
and lightless

(or upon waking,
and forgetting who I am,
or where I am
when seeing the few stars
during an unknowable hour
out the screen
from the top of my tent)

so identity returns by this far
smallness felt between self
and the entirety of the cosmos.

Just as time
can simplify things strange
and complex

(or in closing eyes
to the broken,
pendulumlike
repetition of walnuts
falling and thudding
on the forest floor
around this clearing)

so the distance
of my cosmos
dissolves back into silence

A Thread of Loss

The red and white koi,
the white and red koi
            float
(as if whiskered, flickered
thoughts
navigating surfaces
of reality)
within the circular pond.
The sun is rising.
You hear a few birds beginning to sing,
and the rocky fall
recirculating
an aimlessness.
Anamnesis:
static that peels
away the moments.
Before daybreak,
I woke with tears running down my face,
made coffee,
then walked out here and listened.
I don't know . . .
The sun has risen over the trees.
But the stone
and cinderblock tunnels
of the pond
appear reminiscent of labyrinths
from last night's dream,
where her chimera led my following
into a dark
severed from
Ariadne's Thread.
Without ambit,
those first freedoms
before graceless jealousy
remain fractured from this strange
omen of infinity catching up with me
now.

Catching Up

You chased your imagination west,
through waitressing
and Hollywood,
onto red carpets
where pretty people
get their pictures taken.
You say you visited
the Paris café
where Sartre wrote
and philosophized.
You say you'll be back in town by Thanksgiving.
And I say all the old haunts are tired,
their small places of certainty
filled with a faint sense of loss.

Reflection

While wild turkeys migrate—through woods,
then upon the open circle of a cul-de-sac—
the first word that comes to mind is Thanksgiving,
how the holidays hermeneutically shatter
silences: the year I had walked,
with drink in hand,
through a sliding-glass door.

And there's the same aimless purpose
to these nomadic birds, who meander back
across the yard, the cul-de-sac, and into the woods.
Past a vanishing point's shimmer of time.
As if a stranger knocking at an empty
frame of light, who continues knocking,
until I know again the reflection I answer to.

The Conceit That Unravels into Meaninglessness

In the meantime, I'm living here,
keeping the house in order for showings.
Everything, from the paintings on the walls,
to the furniture on the patio,
has been tagged for sale.

I've been here for weeks.
Just today, I answered the door,
told telemarketers so-and-so
don't live here anymore,
made coffee, smoked a half-dozen cigarettes,
had a beer, and walked the rooms hoping to hear a sound.

A friend once told me
(First, prefacing the advice
by liking it to tombstones
above dead bodies)
what she does when walking into a strange place:
she imagines each face
to be a face of her past—
the young girl who looks up to her mother to speak,
or the teenager with a mouth-full of braces bagging groceries.

But what happens when the faces inside the rooms I enter are owned by dead people?
And I find myself walking past photographs
of this elderly couple,
past their son's paint-by-number pieces
hanging on the walls.
I catch glimpses of myself
from the small mirrors on every wall.
No one is coming here unannounced,
so I can act this way.
Everyone went west after the funeral,
and I can't remember
the original placement of things.

I know the date
only from the newspaper.
I leave the shower running
and fall asleep nude.
Nude, and asleep with the shower running,
I am the pretension of a misplaced object
that has become a conceit
which unravels into meaninglessness.

Anamnesis

But the darkened limitation of one cloud passing
over the tops of redwood pines enveloping
this trail's outer loop is like a self-fluxing by dim,
inner switch—with my subject fading, then returning—
as I recall the recent past when taking this way
during a levelling silence yesterday,
how its repeating difference of Nows, then,
were similar to the decentering dance of light
flickering down upon places to the path
before it bends out of sight, after I've stopped
to sit on a bench appeared between these transient,
disappearing ends, the eerie placelessness
of history here being reminiscent of the few,
unimportant moments this fall,
when I had nothing to gain, nor anything to lose,
and spent too much time in barroom amnesia,
wondering what waiting must feel like.

Imago

Aphorism #2

For what it's worth . . . —Beauty
is a muse with missing laughter.
At times, lightlessly,
appears her borrowed art:
beyond a fence,
there's the reserve
without detail
from a covered porch.

Between the voids of morning dark,
remains an unsaying
I seek without
the echoed dripping
of old snow off eaves,
as if this winter residue

(that is unveiling
in the way
some silences
can be)

was remainder
to the mourning
after my mother
explained to me
her cancer had come back.

And her irreducible will then,
inverts now,
all the illusions
I live on,
the doomed things I don't say,
the false immortalities—
and Death—which is a dawning, rain-riddled
darkness I'm trying

to manage
and push away,
for what it’s worth.

New Year's Day at Shimps Hollow

From out an unnameable silence,
I notice a layer of snow
leftover
from last night
thinly covering tables
surrounding
this firepit.

In watching
orange flames rise,
the crowing of a rooster echoes,
while the sky
lightens violet,
and birds begin singing
in the walnut trees.

Without why,
hours ago I crawled
from a tent into the cold,
forgottenness of a new year,
then welled up some
beside the start
of waking heat and wave.

Here, these seconds pass
as time more novel
than impermanent,
while dawn flickers into being,
and crosses a threshold
I keep between meaning
that can become hope,

or false Resolution.

Take Up Your Bed and Walk

The elision
of the man of much ennui—
months past—who did lie
down (as a nomadic
parenthetical turned
from the world)
on the concrete elevation's
graffiti
underneath this bridge—
which I was passing under
then to pass by
now, over snow and mud
of the trail,
here, in the dead of a listless,
winter quiet—
remains an empty presence
freed from the collective
dream I always feel
as if walking through
its haunt while returning
home.

A Broken Mondo For My Father's Bad Shoulder

The self-ghosts I sought
through to get to now—here   before

the barb-

wire at this farmland end,

while standing beside
my father (who wears a sling,
the hood his thought is hid in,

and another wind-
                        breaker

I helped pull over his arm)
had to die again,
then decompose down to bones,
their haunt like this animal

carcass we've paused by
to talk about, its ribcage
                              curved,

the fragments of fur left near

the fence to acres
of brown grass, with a distant barn
and home beyond. Then, he says

these remains are from
                              a coyote,

though what do I know, what is
dying, anyway? When will

my own ghosts, and their
                              self-

enveloping dark,
come to return? A bright, cold
                                        sky

suspends high over

the feckless field my father
finds to be as far away

as to be or not
to be, but once we've moved on
from its mortal reminder—

and such brief meaning
to being human—the bare
forest lining the fallow

pass forward opens—
as if from my
          memory

of unwrapping the blood-soaked

bandage covering
the holes a surgeon drilled into
                                        his shoulder—

onto a centered
piece of gravel land where paths
encircle, the mementos

people have left behind
here, and their crossroads,
like things healing still from loss.

Open Meaning

Once each morning,
afternoon, and night
some of us would line—
like wordless stanzas—
in the small courtyard,
which was mostly concrete
with some weeds growing through,
and a short, spanish
nurse would light our wheat cigarettes,
handed out from a pack,
then say, "Please,
                    don't blow smoke in my face."

*

My roommate was blind. He reminded me of a character
from an absurdist play, or pictures I'd seen
of a playwright
I couldn't place.

          From the bed,
while reading a book of photographs from *TIME*,
my troubles travelled
from the barred window—
to the old man—
running his hand down
the mystery
of what I thought to be
a white wall's blank image—
this margin which discovered
the door's meaning,
how it had to be
endlessly
open.

The Poem I Planned to Write

From out a Strange, I understood
the slope of stairs,
the still bridge over water

(which I passed upon
into the old beginning
of a poem for karma)

as surface and leaf
under foot my pondering
unwrote, thus, toward a current

fate's decentering.
As if taking a left turn
on the trail (after railing

and board became ground
found mud-thick and slippery)
my thought shifted from homeless,

homeward. Or miles
hence, when crossing shadowed
tracks with a boy in the heart

of adolescence,
who sat as a fatalist
on a bench by his big dog,

the poem I'd planned
went way down another winding
peak,

and into a valley,
then became a piece on non-
interfering with the song

of the suffered earth,
a work which would at times walk
with the quieted woods,

its nature of things,
but also be prosaic—
where my fictions worked against

the fault of their age—
while the narrative of trees
rising up sides of the path

meant more than searching
through the sounds to a storied
future's amor fati,

then, the poem I
had planned to write for empty
winds of fate did discover

choice when following,
by will, undetermined ground
out of a valley's measure.

Imago

Or is such Otherness simply terrifying beauty
existing in a void you can't
live in for long?

On the upclimb
through waning light
and mud-lightened leaves,
there's always the question
beneath the question,
its fleetingness,
a self-lost
with each shadowed moment
back to the real
world.

Middle Paths

The dream I took for miles with
me this morning—
from home,
then through the park and woods—
I awakened to
while passing the stony fathoms
outside a campsite
stuck in shroud.
Of the dwelling
to the dream I remembered
then: a front door
opened to the bright portent of daylight,
while a backdoor led
out into a void of dark.
In this mystical penumbra,
I had wandered through
the subterranean rooms,
from end to end
in a maze of frustration,
without leaving.
But the glimpse I got
of the few tents
behind evergreens,
the smoke spilling from a pit,
and the deep silence—
centered and split
all the meanings
of middle paths
(which I thought
I had known)
into this wide abyss
between self and shadow.
My inner direction
walked farther within
that difference,
until reaching a long,
wooded boardwalk,
where steps echoed out,
without remainder,
after having found ground again.

Apostrophe Poem

Neighbor, this is the hill you meant,
isn't it? Your sledding hill. From here,
the surface plummets
waywardly down . . .
This dam's overflow: it's staked
up to the path by flood-markers. You'd like
the vacuity, how it outlines nothing,
but fills a void,
while expressing that absurd comedy
we try and carry
back uphill with us.
As if the infinite idiocy which carried
your memory one morning
to my apartment.
After snowing for days,
the silent sun had risen.
I remember the feeling
after turning
my rickety knob: loneliness
woven in bright, cold light.
Everything reflectively white.
You with sledding discs under an arm.
And now, walking above this landscape's
bleak canvas of white,
the wind carries isolations,
which collide with your past,
time spent the one winter of building
a motorcycle in the small
square of your living room.
How you eventually pushed
it out into existence.
How you survived
next season's wreck,
but not the road after.

Unexpected Presence

Shoeprints, filled with snow . . .
My own prints on railway boards
leave their emptiness behind.

Ahead, the question
of quarry is half-frozen:
new geese echo through wind.

When I leave the source
and shore back for tracks, shoe-souled
traces end near a treehouse.

A boy, thawing there
between rail and fort, ponders
my unexpected presence.

Novel Ground

Upon my reaching
an expanse
of funneled land,
it's as if nostalgic
residue from a dream
remained in the cracks
of the lost, late morning
light here.

Like an afterthought,
a red fox scampers
from a boundary of trees—
across patches of deadened grass—
into opposing
trees.

This low field reveals last remnants of a storm weeks ago:
snowdrifts,
lingering
ice puddles.

And I recall how the typed,
laminated sign taped
to a storefront
started, "Due to the great blizzard
of this century . . ."

I cross underneath a high bridge.
The road
that it connects
disappears
behind woods
in both directions.

Up there,
two teenage friends
walking along the guardrail
shout down,
signifying certainties of emerged existence,
novel ground.

The Prayer Chapel

When my mother told me her cancer
had come back,
we'd made it
to the pre-silence
of a place on the path
striven in cold,
morning light.

Her will didn't wither,
then, while we walked
from a plain above
the sun-flecked river,
to where words were left over
while snow gusted off
the weed-grass
of a field.

By the time I had sat upon
a backless, stone bench,
she'd gone inside
the tiny chapel
just steps forward
to write down a message,
then strung her prayer
from one of the nails.

Outside, illuminations
slanted across this centered piece of land,
and wind collided
with a quiet's mortal recurrence,
which sunk in
as the chimes
set into the structure
began to sound.

To Tie Back the Threads of Our Unravelling

While atop this hill,
which winds, then unwinds
downward to an access point
where stairs reach up
from a lot's splintered,
wood swing that overlooks the river,
I watch a motorcycle
echo into a space below,
through ashen trees
with branches like old,
cryptic hands.

But the laconic,
spare forest surrounding
the past soon carries
conversation between
a father and son
who have unbounded off the bike.
There's this endless
silence after the man repeats,
"Your mother
and I are getting
a divorce."

After the path passes
over their lasting knot of being
and becomes a bridge
to be crossed over,
I seem to have ceased
questioning the passage
from my own parents' separation,
or the frayed places of peace
we visit in order to tie
back the threads
of our unravelling.

The Leaves That Dance in a Vulnerable Open

From out a network
of paths cleared within the woods
behind home, I soon emerge

onto high ground—
before an old, run-down shack—
the lostness of its structure

which was once, I think,
an outhouse to what is left
of a shelter's splintered frame

some paces farther.
But the stuffed and toy monkey
children from the neighborhood

have hung—by velcroed
paws upside-down on a limb
near part to the paint-chipped

past of this displaced
edifice—is a sodden,
gray and ragged reminder

to the coming spring.
But winter has been dusk light
turning snow the color ash.

Its stark illusion
like the fragment of deadwood
appeared as if suspended

on the frozen white
of Sunfish Pond's shore I paused
before in a waning real.

After lightless weeks,
I walk now under surreal
vines hanging down trees,

out a frame's sheltered otherness,
then into picture and field.
And the bright, expansed wheatfield

swallows such thinking
through my emptying, even,
of the collection to days

spent not by seeking
meaning in destination,
but seeing beauty in things

between, here, where I find
the red gate's forest entrance,
and the leaves beyond,

which are swept up in wind's lost light,
encircling there above
trail ground, their dancing held out

into vulnerable
Open.

Koan #1 at Camp Geronimo

This nightcloud crosses
over the silent, full moon
I watch now through

trunks, limbs and branches
caught in black. Before me, there's
the fugue of flickering light

by a fire's state
of flame and cracking wood. Or
one town from this campground,

a locomotive's
whistling echoes the air.
Once I turn away from such

reverberation,
I see my dog, in the glow
of a headlamp, keeping watch

to the absolute,
empty koan of surrounding
Nature, it reflected back

into her outline.

While at Camp Geronimo When Peeling Back the Rising Light

A morning wheel's
wind gusts through such no-matter
to camp, and sways the sundry

trees starting to leaf
around this clearing. The breeze
blows smoke from a fire (which

cooks breakfast in a
skillet) toward the top of last
night's tent, whose staked-down rain top

flaps from a headwind.
This dawn, I awoke
in the static to birdsong,

gathered wood, then saw
the half-circle of a sun
paused through woods on a skyline

(its light spread thinly
across the horizon) while

my dog meandered
by the picnic table I
stood over, then, to begin

slicing potato
and onion. With the round, white
onionlike sun risen now,

the turning of mid-
day's blustering weather peels
back the past of yesterday's

descent by fire-
light into a thought bottom,
while I sit beside dying,

afternoon embers,
and listen to a silent
swirling that carries my

green focus to growth,

again, filling the forest with
color, the blossoms that shake
like the sound of things

rising, this rising
announcement of Time,
its things beginning to up-

tick.

Scintilla

Aphorism #3

"For sale: baby shoes, never worn". -
While running
through the Sunday ghost
of a town
filled with semblances—
past the bar closed
after a kitchen fire,
then by the old
automotive parts store
turned tattoo parlor—
a phraseology of my phantoms
seems to express,
before I exorcise
the shadow of such
sunless thought,
its myth in Hemingway's six word
short story, "For sale: baby shoes,
never worn."

A couple emerges into the half-light—
out from the florist—with flowers.
When I reach another alley lined by backyards,
an inter-knotting of love and death
links back to images
of her first permanence,
which binds as lack
recognized in symbolic refusal
to the idea of her loss,
uninscribed as a tattoo.
Those fictions return,
as if their nowhereness
were this real crushing under
a universal of gravity,
after I reach the quiet of a cul-de-sac,

where extremes collapse,
then, while walking up
the driveway toward home.

A False Spring

Hints of past existences
lurk around
these tiers of descending,
curved seats
built into the edge
of this field off trail.
My surprise
remains beside
a wood-splintered pulpit
in strange harmonium
amidst such a commingling
of wind and light.
As if beyond frame,
where the amphitheater ends
behind me
sunlight blows through
and through an expanse's drop
off into forest falling
down toward a bottomless
ravine below.
From this threshold,
the displacement of the day
reveals the airy freedoms
of a false spring,
the way its promise
has nothing to add
nor take away.

The Mirror Calm That Returns To Its Source

Rising Waters

The rivers, streamlets,
and creeks off the route
to our way up north are wide

and high, muddied and
mute. Ducklings float on pools
of water collected

in cornfields. This rain's
continuum remains un-
broken when we reach Sucker

Creek (which flows
into Hubbard Lake) after hours
of driving through towns that thinned

for miles until
only dense forest lined roads
singular, the rain we found falling,

still, when reaching the cabin.

A Source's Empty Mirror

As if outside a wheel
of wave and afternoon light,
while watching lakewater

overturn like white whisps
of clouds in low places
across a windy sky,

the smell of firewood
smokes from the cast-iron stove
heating the cabin inside.

From here, I keep no
eye on my father's line reeled out
from a fishing rod left

in the metal
off the dock's
empty boat lift.

Topography of Source

Like circles stretched
from top and bottom, then pulled
inward, or cinched into bays, ends,

and rounded off shorelines,
this wood carving hanging
on the wall beside the glowing stove

shows topographical
depths and points concentric
to Hubbard Lake. If you were

to rotate the frame clock-
wise, the tide blowing in on
stones before the backyard grass

would be Time
to the shore
of Comeback Bay.

The Return

After dinner,
when the lake is glasslike,
I set out walking

in a mirror stilled,
with the dogs, on dirt roads
away from the un-

rippled wake. While
the walking way navigates
sides of thick woods,

I later find (off
lengths to a street as nameless
as my shadow slowly

lessening in the failing
light) the beginning of a
deer reserve's grass path pooled

in places from rainwater.
At the forest field's end,
I seek through this wavering

dark stuck within rows
of ragged pines, to follow trod,
furrowed trails, and their needle-

ground, which discovers
sky over an endless glade,
the dozens of deer frozen there

in twilight,
as if reflections
caught in a calm,

returning heart.

Finding Beatitude

With my beaten
will being broken,
I realize Beauty
after miles of radical reflection,
which have led to this low valley
dotted in purple and white flowers—
and the green beginnings—
along hills as rolling rises
between two steep climbs.

And there's natural rapture
in the stream running across the way,
silent measure in stones
stepped upon while I further
into the exhaustion
of an inner finitude
known now by this late, repeating light—
falling onto the impulses of nature—
as if veils from eyes.

After navigating around the angled
vision of a photographer,
who seems to be searching pathway
toward presence beyond image,
I pass over the sand and skeleton
of a dried-up creek bed,
to find beatitude when climbing
this narrow ascension
lined by wildflower.

Dogwood Pond

Paused at this overview,
the will is akin to wind
through a doorway:
an imageless succession
of empty frames.

After, trees that line
the descent are creaking,
old doors closing
behind rooms
of static landscape.

The pond, then,
at the foot
of the hillock
is mirrorlike,
a source to searching
through unrealized absence—
off one dirt path
to shore
bog water,
reeds.

Hovering there, distortedly,

reflects a Narcissus inverted—
unnamable,
irreducible.

Past, Current, River Past

The fragments of white that flashed
across the window last night,
and the sheets and sheets

of rain that howled
against shuttered glass,
in part runs

the river I've reached—
this evening—ochre and wide.
The wide water rushes by,

and ebbs up
to where I've paused
on sand-turned-mud

beside a bridge's column.
Around curving concrete
is tagged in graffiti:

The Green Gang Was Here,

here, being beside a concrete
column somewhere in Ohio,
miles from last night's past,

its stormwind,
with the dogs scratching
to get inside my room,

the two pawing back
in without the black,
gray-whiskered shepherd

we had to put down
days ago.

Hiccups

At one of the last Blockbusters,
my buddy, who wasn't the rewind guy,
vanished, to reappear

while I was in line—
stolen bottles of Jägermeister
hid underneath his jeans.

He led the way back—
clankingly—
to the clinic,

where everyone got drunk
eventually,
and breathalyzed.

The nurses,
who'd drain the boil
on my backside afternoons,

couldn't cure his hiccups,
which continued all night
from across the hall,

echoing, still, after a lady
on the late shift relayed
to him her sugar packet remedy.

As a Customer on the Covered Bridge

The township
has censored the graffiti
on a railing
running past this bench.

Two barefoot,
orphaned girls
kick water,
killing time
below
my waiting over the creek.

And I find the truck
we pushed from
its marked-for-towed fate,
rusting still
in one of the bridge's
spaces.

*

He emerges
around the street corner
and into the quiet.

Down the quiet street he skateboards,
these dark glasses dulling the light,
and the two girls
disappear around
a creek bend.

Diner Mosaic

Sirens begin
their bellows;
a waitress taps
thoughts of
Elsewhere
upon a bar.

*

Across from her,
Rooster starts
up again: "Storm must be coming,"
and, "Seen myself
on the news last night."

*

Kitschy paintings,
from a variety of artists,
hang for sale on the walls.

*

Near the profiled portrait
of a provincial
horse's head, light—
coming from a window
onto my table—
darkens.

*

"Where'd you get those?"
I hear the waitress,
torn between surprise
and amusement,
ask Rooster.

*

A cook
wearing an apron
emerges
out the kitchen's

swinging doors . . .

*

Kitschy paintings,
from a variety of artists,
hang for sale on the walls.

*

Beyond the counter
and the waitress
taking my check,
through a long glass window,
muted rain
pantomimes
the empty street.

*

Turning in a barstool,
Rooster says
to us: "Stormin' now."

He unhooks,
holds up these
handcuffs
and determines: "Sheriff gave me
them yesterday."

*

Kitschy paintings,
from a variety of artists,
hang for sale on the walls.

Elegy

Months went by.
Fall turned-up
its collar to winter.

It got so cold
I walked next-door
to my neighbor's apartment
and asked to borrow
his space heater.

He said something—
slipped away—
then reappeared,
like a quotation without text.

*

At those rent places,
each space had a square plot of land,
a little wooden fence.

After the season changed again,
the man drove in pink,
plastic flamingos
up to his door.

Later, he planted a few
thorny,
red roses.

*

One day,
I was reading something on my step
when he hung a sign outside,
which said, "Do not disturb."

It wound around the knob, as if
flicking sunlight.

Along with the everyday light,
he disappeared back
into his apartment.

Rainy Dithyramb

The shadow of a sky's
questions were answered
sometime after the outpouring
of our dawn treading led, suddenly,
into the stillness of a forest's upclimb.
Beyond the continuous, unconditional
banter between my mother and I,
thunder groaned from a source
we couldn't see:
everywhere the light fluxed.

So sheets from the storm blew
through the canopies and soaked us.
The water streamed across places
where the ascent levelled to stones.
Soon, our echoing reached image . . .
From this opening, as if at a threshold
separating dream and reality,
hovered a field of wheat
I had wanted to show her.
Under trees, we stood and watched.

Empty Hooks

Two friends fish a part
to the river under Route
725's concrete

bridge (one friend wading
with line cast, while the other
stands in the stones and sand off

shore). A walking man
outlined in black, and paint-stamped
underneath cars echoing

overhead, signifies
the path back home. But pausing
here, my dog laps the water,

evening wanes, the last
of the setting light remains
like haphazard words reeling in

empty hooks, time, sighs.

Boy #3

It was after the omen of birds, all season
flying into windows
and paralyzing themselves,
then, the pileated woodpecker,
who chose a section of roof
to hammer away at each morning,
after I crawled through the upstairs
bedroom window
to nail a red ribbon there,
or, after the dog
uprooted a burrow of baby cottontails,
them fleeing and being flung
by her out of the grass—
the two surviving I took in,
both hid half-alive in a rose bush
though they passed anyway
days later—
after this bucolic chain of broken events
I was led to a sort
of understanding
for the natural world
from a girl in soiled clothes,
kind and dumb,
in a town boarded up still
following a tornado.
I chanced upon her,
browsing the "Pets" section of Craigslist,
looking for closure
within the chaos
of a mangled order,
to be eventually handed
the wrong,
Jefferson Airplane
white one
from her grainy
photographs,
Boy #3.

They live ten years,
you can grab him
like this,
she said stonily.

The Undercurrent of Quiet Everywhere

The horses
let out to graze beyond
the fence I walk along
toward home
appear in a hovering,
simple dusk.

Where the farm fence ends,
grass becomes sand
leading along
the river
and beneath
a bridge.

When surface turns to hard earth
I emerge, through trees,
onto the backroad
of a concrete plant's
after-hour
dormancy.

The gravel lot where
workers park is emptied
of the vehicles it held
on my flight
to High View
earlier.

And all day
this undercurrent of darkness
I cannot explain
has been pulling my fate
through the twilit state
of a fading static.

Here, quiet absorbs
the machines and mountains of material,
as if outer veils were swallowed
into an inner absence
reflected everywhere,
inside-out.

Pre-silence

The thud behind, and another
somewhere off the way,
then a squirrel bounces,
over debris and felled trees,
to gather a nut.

And I'd like to believe
in the mystical notion
that the soul is composed
of the same presence
connecting these surroundings.

The blue and black butterfly
who alights, from mud marked
in partial shoeprints,
onto the old fragment
of a wire-rusted fence.

But after climbing a dirt divide
I'd always trekked blindly by,
there's this vacant sense
of a civilization
moving restlessly on.

More and more,
my machinations have been leading
to unmoored places,
as if metaphorical rebirths
into a past no longer mine.

Through leaf and branch
I emerge into a pre-silence,
or the term I use to signify
a return of self
to reincarnation.

As if the constant
futures of change
were stilled to a point
of finding again
a beginning.

Above this clearing,
a steel sky mists down.
A fire smolders,
the smoke flooding
out an iron-cased pit.

The Sigh of Simplifying

Like a Thoreau
searching through the void
to another experience
existing
between the rustic and rational,
these simplified bits
of discarded reality
around the train tracks
I walk along
on way to the trail,
entail: the empty box to a pregnancy test,
crushed cans,
effaced containers . . .

In passing, I consider
a civilization incarnated
(as if by the locomotive
the author could hear
from his cabin)
or in echo of the image
absent yet heard,
the idea of a silence
displaced after I descend
down to the disquieted ditch
off the road of determinate cars,
then into the opening
of a wooded otherness.

The way this difference
leaves lassitudes
of little significance,
for enveloping entrance
into simplicity
of path and river,
seems to return
my complexities of conviction
to origins before fixed motive:
toward a time when I could pause
and enjoy reading the graffiti
under a bridge
before moving on.

Scintilla

The empty spark
of this sun-faded road,
which remains vastly husked
from flatland and cornfield,
is lined by quieted thrash
passing outside the window,
where the profile of my dog
hangs partially
in the rushing wind.

Through an opening in the woods,
I turn off onto a gravel
and tire-grooved drive's
transfiguring distance,
as if these lengths
driven farther into forest
were to lead from the last remnants
of reality and content lost,
to form empty but contented.

When this narrow passage
enveloped by green form
frees to clearing,
I park there in the unreality,
then wander into the afterimage
of walnuts fallen from trees,
which cover completely,
by echoing traces,
the surrounding campground.

While stopping at orange cigarette butts,
flickered like ash of a past light
left in this firepit,
a hiker happens into camp
from a frontcountry path,
the rucksack on her back
filled with contents and curiosity,
on her face a scintilla
of caution toward my own happening.

Navigating the Darkness

This pre-dawn toil
I know my waking will
stands on its own in,
or after having left a tent
for the open question of morning dark,
I guess around
and navigate the way to coffee,
with the static light of a headlamp
projecting upon forest
and other possessions left out.

Once the dispersion
of my illuminations
find the bunsen burner
on a wood-warped table,
I soon listen
to water boiling,
while a moth hovers in and out
the source shining,
as if a third, blurred eye,
from forehead.

From the soil
this square of searching light
partially falls on,
an insect flies up to collide
with the face of my lamp,
by which I'm trying to sketch
Time into a notebook
laid on the bowed bench
below the table
where water boils on a burner.

As if in semblance
to the black and white
of morning habit,
I rise to pour the hot contents
into a cup's coffee mix,
then measure the distance my light

can make through the nearby wood,
and consider what, exactly, exists out there
in the silence for my dog to be sitting
so expectantly before its darkness.

Muse II

You were sitting on a park bench,
somewhat smiling
at the entire thing,
pale and constant
like a world
had been resolved,
but happy in the way
a mutable heart
cannot both at once
forget and be
remembered by.

Harvest

Aphorism #4

What's in a name? —When the surface levels,
the weathered tree
of one hundred names
rises at a place,
before I begin
to realize existence again,
from which all turns
away from futures.

The trunk
is engraved as detail
in eternal repetition
of initials and dates,
a myriad of etchings
that elaborate
a return
to time.

What the season lends now
is a windless and dusty unchaining,
an unchainment
of the nameless, mohawked youth
who remained sitting by the tree
while smoking cigarettes
on my trekking past
to the meadow.

Upon circling back here
home after miles through
rolling wheatgrass,
the traces of old butts and beer cans
reveal that unnamable void
between our forms of empty convention,
and the meanings we seek
in substance away from definition.

Spectrum From Campsite H-14

When gleaning upward
from my seat, two bent pines
lean into one another

before becoming canopies. I

watch the white clouds move
across blue sky, watch the sun
fall through, layering other

oak leaves yellow. A bluesome

boy walks behind his mother
(her rolling a wagon
of things) while he

drags a sack, gray as a middle way,

over the gravel path
that divides sides
to this campground.

A dog barks.

At the site beside mine,
clothes hang
on a line tied between trees.

From another square of land,

a lady snaps, then spreads a colorful
cloth
over her picnic table.

Backwards Projection

During dawn's next day, I drive
through the bluegreen of sky and rolling hills,
this rural byway, home. Leaving is always

the simple part. Its detachment like looking
into a rearview mirror, but seeing afterimage
and sign selling firewood on a receding road.

And yesterday, there was the waking,
primitive noise of night, its dark and difficult
otherness of people beginning

their shadows around fires. ...The tercet
of old, childhood friends walked by
my campsite again, as if backwards in time,

with bundles of plastic wrapped wood,
then much later, a remaining man
paced up and down the gravel length,

which split the quiet sites in half,
a cone of muttering light
projecting his steps.

Finding Freedom

My bits of truth in every fiction—or my
bits of fiction in every truth—
recognize
now
the few buildings

(their likenesses
as if elevated
apostrophes
claiming ownership
of civilization
            and its watchful rule)

which rise over this field of trees
while I trek back from
the pathos of the paths of Daniel's Peace,
its long corridorlike entrance lined with pines
that unwove, then,
            feeling
back to a thread's
acceptance for the rags of time-
spent in looking
for a self-ceased,
after mania's convergence
of love and death,
at an asylum's interrupted
world.

By convergence of love and death,
I mean that the bits of truth
in fiction—
or the bits of fiction in truth—
remain as this jarring
simplicity of people
sitting on benches,
or walking in pairs,
at the park behind the buildings
when reaching the realities of lengthening shadows,
with the respite I've sought
finding freedom
in the last of the light here.

A Homonym of Routes

"To return to the root is to find peace."
—Lao Tzu, "Tao Teh Ching"

As if two people spelled differently.
But the route of this barefoot lady,
and my similar sounding wordlessness,
will cross once more
at a point somewhere
on the circular trail
between valley and peak.

There are routes to the roots
ripping from the earth of this hill.
A map of common ground.
When I glance back up from tree-root-stairs,
the face of a bluff
across space
is without direction.

During the uprooting of thought and place,
I understand
a routeless feeling.
Or: there's the rootless
way I find myself
in the strained
sense of losing touch.

Routes converge
when the lady descending
down wraps her arm
around a warped tree,
navigating the surface
by it in careful steps.

Like someone walking in time,
she touches the bill to her hat,
says, "Hi again,"
then returns to the root of a surface
in search of peace,
which exists perhaps in homonym
or harmony of difference.

The Idea of Dissipation

The morning rain falling through trees—
then onto the long,
dried up creek bed's
stone and bedrock,
which I'm finding a footing down—
murmurs around conversation
between myself
and an English lady in raincoat,
her paused
now at an echo's-distance
above me on this slope
from hiking with her two dogs.

The accent of dialogue
falls on charming,
or care freed from confusion
and any history.
The big Idea I carry
after our talking
is this good as Platonic
soul that links
forward to my own dog,
who leads the way to where
a current connects
at a base of intersections.

*

In continuum,
the nameless, omniscient weather
collides and ripples with a river
I watch while walking along a field's
high, root-exposed drop.
And the way this space
unearths the impossible essence
within all things around
is akin to a kind of distance
between strangers
that dissipates
out here.

Couplets Open to a Way Out of Appearances

And then this dried up creeklet, its hollowed
out stone and old leaf, this burnt ground

of split, dirt earth I trek until reaching
a stark sky's looping powerlines.

When scanning sides of scythed, unrolling hills
that hold electrical towers in metered circuit,

current is repeating image without beginning
or end, a Between in a continuum.

After opening, faceless time turns on its boot,
surrounding space becomes forest.

And the pair I find sitting on a bench,
near the peak of a steep upclimb—

the lady with long, silver-streaked hair,
and the boy with his map unfolded—

look to one another, then ask me the way
out of Appearances:

All of this seems the same,
All of this seems the same,

the boy says.

Ellipsis

After passing over a footbridge,
then through the repeating
quiet of a forest—
which sticks like static
to the compass of my interior—
I soon wander upon a recurring,
identical bridge.

Image overlaps image
before I return to the surface
of a meadow's
gold-tipped,
waving wheatgrass,
with black blooms
belatedly there in the Is.

And time
dissolves terrain
into strangeness,
until my forgetting
returns
to the ellipsis
of another forest's footbridge.

Incarnated,
as an uncanny question
just come into reality,
is the man absently turning
within his hands
a long piece of the landscape
I've recently drifted through.

Caesura

As the wide river I walk along runs
silent through evening forest, time
passes as time wends when its cyclical
limit has nowhere to turn but around
and around, like water chasing its current,
with my own moments caught now,
by undertow, before the climb
of this windless, broken rock passage
I peer up into . . .

The floating shade, and fragments of dusty
matter are hung in static above an earth
split and overturned, the revolving world
of these divided seconds like the caesura
this morning between the dark outside
a gas mart, then the fluorescent lighting
inside, the upclimb of the mother sliding
coins across the counter for a package
of powdered doughnuts,

the small line growing behind her.

Trail Notes in Haiku

The burnt orange and white
of a dead fox remains by
a worn forest pass

A small girl holds
two branches of withered leaves
while walking with dad

(As if wild blooms
waving as One in a wind
that rolls through grassland)

One somewhat antlered,
and a knee-knobby fawnling,
cross this gravel road

The stalks of these sun-
flowers rise as likenesses to a
sister's laugh

My dog almost lies
down in a stream ankle deep,
but sits there instead

A past girl lost
in her phone is not unfound
when we cross trailways

What moves me from mind
along a river timeless
and silent and felt?

It's dawn, and the still
smallness of the dead fox found
yesterday is gone

Overnight Mythopoetic

Dionysus withdraws into Apollo.
Earlier, the unfamiliar echo
of speeding boats off lakewater

had a likeness to the strange
wine of displacement
felt when returning

from the trail
to two transient
friends waiting

on motorcycles
at my campsite
lot.

The whine
of their riding away
was afterimage. After image,

I watched my dog
roll around in grass
while cooking lunch on a grate

over wood. Tonight,
while sitting up inside
a tent staked down

on grassland close
to a pond shoreline,
I read by headlamp

and listen to nameless fish
splashing in darkness.
Words trail off this page

like faint music drifting
in from somewhere distant . . .
The open sense of an earth

turning homelessly
diminishes to irreducible origin,

dims.

Dead Metaphor at Hopewell Backpack Camp

This morning,
as steam escaped from a metal pot
boiling water,

a heron, looking for breakfast,
descended through
the treetops

and landed on deadwood
stuck end-up
in a pond

at the far edge
to this campground clearing.
The moon, hung in the lightening sky,

soon disappeared with the sun.
For some time,
I sat at a picnic table,

turned toward the mirrored water,
and watched
the reflection

of a question
concerning metaphor dead
to time's aimless

Red Herring,
its hunted mystery finished
when the bird flew away

without food
while I sipped
coffee.

Finding a Curve of Days

I.

This lavender sky
the color of wild lilacs
wavering in a field
whose boundary I walk along.

Or there's omen in the lavender sky
from stormwind colliding against chimes
hanging from the post
of a boundary fence.

Past the song
blowing from wind chimes sounding,
I find a walking stick
buried in whirring grass.

By the returning paces
upon surface with this warped stick,
wavering sky becomes stilled shadow
while I hurriedly take a forest path home.

II.

This worn-smooth walking stick
left leaning against a tree
at the base of the path upward,
and through forest, I grasp.

Or out of the radical solitude of home,
there's certainty in the expanse and breath
upon emerging from under
overhanging limbs.

Here, the light of afternoon sky
is the color of wild,
yellow coneflowers stilled in the field
whose boundary I walk.

So the semi-split center of these days
lifts and ingathers steps
past the windless chimes
of a cemetery fencepost.

III.

As if by a curve of days,
this walking stick remains warped
from the manifold strangers
who have grasped it.

Or the piece of this faded moon
hanging in the light blue of evening
is akin to the bent
of time spent setting up here.

Under a setting sky,
the light sinking behind trees
is my ingathered rhythm of thuds
around the field of late coneflowers and lilacs.

And the wide horizon I walk under
is the shape of this walking stick,
when taken from soil,
then up lengthwise into my hand.

The Pages of Glacier Point

Set free from its indifference,
the afternoon sky—
bright and emptied
of cloud and meaning—
is image passing
into being as evening
steeling blue,
and wisped
with streaks of late,
pinkish light.

With the sky setting free
words indifferent
to pages of light,
I glimpse from my reading
while lying supine
in a hammock
tied between two trees,
at the edge of this overlook's
view of miles
to field beyond.

From shutting sentences
of sky and field distantly
darkening beyond
punctuation,
I pocket the horizon of my pages,
then take up a walking stick
left leaning against a tree,
and set out—
through dusk's difference—
homeward.

In such gloaming light,
indifference freed
now are these deer
leaping through high grass
and flower of a field—
then into the landscape

of black trees—
disappearing
as if in the moment
of their pages.

Harvest

Tin cans
left on roadside shacks
fill with change,
quarters for sweet corn.
Green afternoons,
farmers ride down
the bleached town roads
on tractors.
Cars collect,
one by one,
behind a harvest
of days.

Acknowledgments

Alexandria Quarterly: Catching Up, Harvest

All Existing Literary Magazine: Aphorism #1, Aphorism #4, The Sigh of Simplifying

Amethyst Review: Finding Beatitude

Carcinogenic Anthology II: The Conceit That Unravels into Meaninglessness

Cerasus Poetry Magazine: Unexpected Presence

Hole in The Head Review: Asylum, Dogwood Pond

Mizmor Anthology: As a Customer on the Covered Bridge

Nebulous Magazine: A Thread of Loss

North by Northeast Literary Magazine: The Passing That Never Is, Up North

On-the-High Literary Review: A False Spring

Poetry as Promised Magazine: Apostrophe Poem, Take Up Your Bed and Walk, The Prayer Chapel, To Tie Back the Threads of Our Unravelling

Superpresent: Elegy

The Basilisk Tree: Aphorism #2, Aphorism #3

Unleash Lit: Koan #1 at Camp Geronimo, The Leaves That Dance in a Vulnerable Open, While at Camp Geronimo When Peeling Back the Rising Light

Willows Wept Review: Finding a Curve of Days

Written Tales: Caesura

www.ingramcontent.com/pod-product-compliance
Lightning Source LLC
LaVergne TN
LVHW090534110826
845146LV00003B/1087

* 9 7 9 8 8 9 9 9 0 3 6 0 1 *